YOUR KNOWLEDGE HAS VALUE

- We will publish your bachelor's and master's thesis, essays and papers

- Your own eBook and book - sold worldwide in all relevant shops

- Earn money with each sale

Upload your text at www.GRIN.com
and publish for free

Is the "Criminal Minds" character Spencer Reid a typical genius?

Bibliographic information published by the German National Library:

The German National Library lists this publication in the National Bibliography; detailed bibliographic data are available on the Internet at http://dnb.dnb.de.

ISBN: 9783346765017
This book is also available as an ebook.

© GRIN Publishing GmbH
Nymphenburger Straße 86
80636 München

All rights reserved

Print and binding: Books on Demand GmbH, Norderstedt, Germany
Printed on acid-free paper from responsible sources.

The present work has been carefully prepared. Nevertheless, authors and publishers do not incur liability for the correctness of information, notes, links and advice as well as any printing errors.

GRIN web shop: https://www.grin.com/document/1298369

Oberstufenjahrgang
2017 / 2019

SEMINARARBEIT

Rahmenthema des wissenschaftspropädeutischen␣Semin0ars:
Crime Fiction
Leitfach: Englisch

Thema der Arbeit: Is the Criminal Minds character Spencer Reid a typical genius?

Abgabetermin: 06. November 2018

Table of Contents

1. What is a genius?... 3
2. The term "typical genius".. 3
   - 2.1 General definition... 3
   - 2.2 Historical meaning 4
   - 2.3 Current significance 5
3. Characterisation of Spencer Reid 6
   - 3.1 Introduction to the series 6
   - 3.2 Character traits and properties.. 6
   - 3.3 Individual type of determination 7
   - 3.4 Social Awkwardness 8
     - 3.4.1 Autistic leanings 8
     - 3.4.2 Asperger Syndrome 8
4. Comparison 9
   - 4.1 Similarities between Spencer Reid and a typical genius 9
     - 4.1.1 Considering the general definition 9
     - 4.1.2 Considering the historical meaning 10
     - 4.1.3 Considering the current significance 11
   - 4.2 Differences between Spencer Reid and the typical genius 11
     - 4.2.1 Considering the general definition 11
     - 4.2.2 Considering the historical meaning 12
     - 4.2.3 Considering the current significance 12
   - 4.3 Final word... 13
5. References 14

1. What is a genius?

"Talent is a flame. Genius is a fire"[1] – Bernard Williams

This quotation represents my understanding of the term genius before my researches started. Of course, no one questions terms that are familiar to them, but the more it is dealt with the closer one gets to the real meaning behind these terms. For example, Bernard Williams claims that a genius is the increase to a talented person which leads to the question whether a genius is a remarkable person because of his hard work or just because he is gifted. This is one of the questions dealt with in these term papers and beyond the concept of a genius is also defined. Therefore, the typical genius based on historical and current influences is compared with the above-average intelligent Criminal Minds character Doctor Spencer Reid, related to his character traits and properties, as well as his individual type of determination and his Social Awkwardness.

2. The term "typical genius"

2.1 General definition

First, based on Encyclopaedia Britannica, there are two possible ways of understanding the term genius.

> "In the first sense, as popularized by [Lewis Madison] Terman, it refers to great intellectual ability as measured by performance on a standardized intelligence test. In the second and more popular sense, as derived from [...] Sir Francis Galton, it designates creative ability of an exceptionally high order as demonstrated by actual achievement"[2]

So according to the first meaning the only property of a genius is to perform better in a standardized test than the mass which suggests that only a higher intelligence is expected of him. But it also shows that highly intelligent people tend to be loner because they are extraordinary and their qualities distinguish them from the masses. Their outstanding properties do not fit in the rather one-sided thinking society. It starts with thinking beyond the borders. Moreover, these people are usually not scared to accept the fact that they do not know

---

[1] BrainyMedia Inc 2018, "Bernard Williams Quotes",
https://www.brainyquote.com/quotes/bernard_williams_379649 accessed on 28.10.2018
[2] Kerr, Barbara "Genius" https://www.britannica.com/science/genius-psychology released on 20.07.1998, accessed on 11.10.2018

everything while a very common reflex for an average person is to pretend as if he knew exactly what he is talking about as a defence reaction because he is afraid to get called stupid. But a genius likes to expand his knowledge. Being open-minded can make an enormous impact on smart persons learning skills since they do not close themselves off to new ideas or experiences. Furthermore, I would also like to concentrate on the creative part combined with the achievement of new advances. A genius does not only deal with what already exists, but also has the ability to think beyond it. The genius discovers or invents new things as his ideas transcend our way of thinking. This creativity of creation shows that the genius is not afraid to enter undiscovered areas and to explore the unexplored.

2.2 Historical meaning

In the "Storm and Stress" era (1776-1785), poets began to focus on a main character, who was either a genius or a hero. The philosophers wanted to clarify this previously vague concept of genius. One of these philosophers was Johann Casper Lavater (1741-1801) who wrote "Physiognomische Fragmente" (Physiognomic Fragments) in order to have the possibility of deducing the character of a person from their external appearance. In the beginning he starts with a definition to characterise the appearance and qualities of a genius:

" [...] Wer bemerkt, wahrnimmt, schaut, empfindet, denkt, spricht, handelt, bildet, dichtet, singt, schafft, vergleicht, sondert, vereinigt, folgert, ahndet, gibt, nimmt – als wenn's ihm ein Genius, ein unsichtbares Wesen höherer Art diktiert oder angegeben hätte, der hat Genie; als wenn er selbst ein wesen höherer Art wäre – ist Genie. [...] "
[3]

It may sound odd that an invisible creature gives one advises but the key aspect is that a genius acts so different than from what a normal human being could ever imagine. Further interpretations of this quotation are that this connection between the genius and the being of a higher kind is on a different level than the area of understanding goes. Their mind can open up to another level of knowledge to which normal people have no access. Besides it is also important to mention that Lavater categorizes the features of a genius. There are intellectual habitudes like intelligence, speech faculty and judgement, but also emotional habitude like sentiments, and creative and artist habitudes like poetizing and singing, and social habitudes like giving and taking. Just being smart does not make you a genius. Moreover, Lavater also

---

[3] Cornelsen Deutschbuch 10. Klasse Gymnasium Bayern, 9. Sturm und Drang – Junge Stimmen gegen Autoritäten S.198 Z.15ff.

wrote an explanation on which it may be possible to recognize a genius because "[...] Wo Wirkung, Kraft, Tat, Gedanke, Empfindung ist, die von Menschen nicht gelernt und nicht gelehrt werden kann, da ist Genie! [...] Genie – propior Deus [...] "[4]. This means that a genius does not behave like a normal person because he does not feel and think as society has taught him. This statement confirms the theory that a genius was not born extraordinary, but only through his unique way of thinking he became a genius. There is also a less common expression, the term propior Deus, which is Latin and is translated as the second God. Two fictional layers are used to illustrate this idea: One on which the average population can only learn limited knowledge and above a higher class. On this level the genius is equated with God who is known for his omniscience. In summary, it can be said that Lavater sees the genius above the average population and on a level that is inaccessible to them.

2.3 Current significance

Nevertheless, people are more likely to believe in scientific evidence of intelligence these days. The newspaper "Die Zeit" wrote about the modern understanding of the term genius:

> " [...] Studien zeigen: Menschen, die wir als genial betrachten, haben manches mitgebracht, als sie zur Welt kamen. Intelligenz etwa, oder Temperament. Vieles andere mussten sie sich erkämpfen. Die Analyse gibt Aufschluss darüber, welche Faktoren Menschen zu Genies werden ließen. Bildung, Kreativität, Inspiration, Intuition, Unabhängigkeit, Beharrlichkeit und Glück sind sieben wesentliche Zutaten für jene, die sich anschicken, die Welt zu verändern – und sie sind allesamt eher irdischer Natur."[5]

Looking at this newspaper clipping, it is important to point out that people who society sees as geniuses are often born with basic skills such as intelligence or temperament. But these abilities do not turn people into geniuses. A human being must fight all his life to attain all the other qualities. The composition of factors which are according to Andreas Sentker education, creativity, inspiration, intuition, independence, persistence and luck is what makes a person a genius. These qualities are attainable for every normal person. But to have these "ingredients" as essential character traits it must be either be a big coincidence or hard work on one's being because to train these traits like intuition or independence requires patience and great will. And

---

[4] Cornelsen Deutschbuch 10. Klasse Gymnasium Bayern, 9. Sturm und Drang – Junge Stimmen gegen Autoritäten S.198 Z.24ff.
[5] Sentker, Andreas, "Genial! ", https://www.zeit.de/2011/42/Genie-Kult/komplettansicht released on 13.10.2011, accessed on 24.09.2018

even if a person tries to achieve this degree of perfection in his character the last "ingredient" luck is not determined by the will of the person. Therefore, one must assume that a human being has to learn all his life and work hard on himself in order to perhaps acquire these abilities of a genius.

3. Characterisation of Spencer Reid
3.1 Introduction to the series

Someone who has been learning and working hard all his life is the Criminal Minds character Doctor Spencer Reid, but it remains to be seen if he has achieved the abilities of a genius. Firstly, Criminal Minds is an American television series which is categorized as crime fiction because it is police procedural. There are altogether 14 seasons however I am limiting myself to the first one. The main supervisory agents are Jason Gideon, Aaron Hotchner, Elle Greenaway, Derek Morgan, Doctor Spencer Reid, Jennifer Jareau and Penelope Garcia. The plot is set in Quantico in Virginia. Criminal Minds shows the investigations of a group of behavioural profilers who work for the Federal Bureau of investigation (FBI) as members of their Behavioural Analysis Unit (BAU). The investigators focus on the previous approach and the psychological background of the criminal to solve the case. They are commissioned when a murder has already happened and then investigate it for special characteristics of the criminal's actions. A perpetrator profile is adapted based on the previous results and on the typical serial killer. The profilers try to put themselves in the perpetrator's place to understand their actions. When it comes to dangerous situations it is their strategy to talk to the criminals and calm them down to de-escalate and give them a chance to show remorse.

3.2 Character traits and properties
When it comes to Spencer Reid's intelligence he "[does not] believe that intelligence can be quantified, but [he has] an IQ of 187, an eidetic memory and [he] can read 20.000 words per minute"[6] so one can assume that he has the possibility to work faster and more efficiently than people who are not that gifted. These are the measurable talents with which he is born and which he has as basic unlearned abilities. His professional success so far has been his three doctorates[7] and he also has a broad background knowledge which he can access immediately

---

[6] Criminal Minds, Season 1, Episode 1, 11:00
[7] Cf. Criminal Minds, Season 1, Episode 1, 10:55

at any time. Special Agent Hotchner once introduced Spencer as "Doctor Reid, our expert on, well, everything"[8] what underlines on the one hand his seemingly unlimited knowledge and on the other hand the agent's confidence that Spencer has never said anything wrong before. At the beginning of the series Spencer Reid is 23 years old and because of his outstanding achievements with this young age "people see [him] as a kid"[9]. Special Agent Jason Gideon's solution for this problem is to always introduce Spencer as "Doctor Spencer Reid" and not as a normal "Special Agent" so "he wants to make sure that [the people] respect [him]"[10].

3.3 Individual type of determination

The most important aspect that characterizes Criminal Minds and distinguishes it from other crime series is that the focus is laid on the criminal's psychology and his mental disorders rather than the process of investigation. Doctor Reid got taught by Special Agent Jason Gideon that "the only truly effective weapon we have is our ability to do the one thing they can't. [...] Empathize. They dehumanize their victims. We humanize the killers"[11]. The profilers find and outwit the criminals with the help of their special tactics by trying to understand their actions and their thought process. Doctor Spencer Reid calls this method "psychoanalyze crime scenes in order to gain better understanding of the criminal who might have committed the crime"[12]. The psychological depths of the criminals are explored and their current actions are related to their childhood and past traumas. Spencer Reid relies on the fact that he can beat a criminal with the created profile by knowing his psychological composition and therefore relies on this and not on a gun. The thinking that "you don't need a gun to kill somebody"[13] also makes him stand out from the normal investigators. Since with the characteristics of a typical serial killer and its average behaviour one can usually say a lot about the current criminal, but of course one must compare these precision cases with the current case and might encounter possible discrepancies. To perform this tactic perfectly Spencer Reid had to learn the talent of thinking "outside the box"[14]. Due to Reid's eidetic memory, he can recite any statistic at any time, but he had to learn that one can not only rely on the statistics, but also has to remember that every case is special and individual. While investigating it is an advantage to have a pattern to follow

---

[8] Criminal Minds, Season 1, Episode 1, 08:30
[9] Criminal Minds, Season 1, Episode 1, 25:40
[10] Criminal Minds, Season 1, Episode 1, 25:40
[11] Criminal Minds, Season 1, Episode 6, 15:20
[12] Criminal Minds, Season 1, Episode 18, 02:10
[13] Criminal Minds, Season 1, Episode 6, 38:35
[14] Criminal Minds, Season 1, Episode 2, 25:55

for example that one familiarizes himself with the files first and then looks at the scene of crime and questions the witnesses and suspicious. But to understand the psyche of a killer Spencer Reid had to learn to put himself in the position of somebody who is extremely driven by a motive like revenge or a coercive disturbance that the one has not seen any other way to do as a murder.

3.4 Social Awkwardness

3.4.1 Autistic leanings

Doctor Spencer Reid is a specialist in being able to empathize with the mental illnesses and disorders as he himself has a problem with Social Awkwardness. The first mental disorder that is mentioned in the series are the "autistic leanings of the very insecure Dr. Reid"[15]. Autism is a psychological illness with which a person "challenges with social skills, repetitive behaviors, speech and nonverbal communication"[16]. In simple terms the interaction with other people is frequently difficult because he does not understand the social conditions and manners that belong to a conversation. For example, Spencer often focuses on topics that are not interesting for the other participants, but he does not realize that he should either stop talking about it or change the subject. Another situation in which one could guess his Autism is when Spencer was asked by Special Agent Hotchner to speak to students who were about his age. Spencer was stammering and felt visibly uncomfortable as the centre of their attention. By being set under this pressure he also could not focus on the important pieces of information instead he just puts many technical terms together[17].

3.4.2 Asperger Syndrome

The Asperger Syndrome is a development disorder which leads to "social impairment with extreme egocentricity, limited interests and […] non-verbal communication problem[s]"[18]. All these descriptions apply to Spencer Reid because it is difficult for him to get out of his own mind and adapt to the customs of society. When he is enthusiastic about something it is hard

---

[15] Criminal Minds, Season 1, Episode 5, 31:50
[16] 2018 Autism Speaks Inc., "What is Autism?", https://www.autismspeaks.org/what-autism accessed on 27.10.2018
[17] Cf. Criminal Minds, Season 1, Episode 2, 18:00
[18] ©1996-2018 MedicineNet, Inc., "Medical Definition of Asperger syndrome", https://www.medicinenet.com/script/main/art.asp?articlekey=9675#aspergers_syndrome_facts reviewed on 25.01.2017, accessed on 27.10.2018

for him to drop the subject even when he annoys his colleagues with it. Sometimes Spencer must be stopped by the other investigators when he starts talking about topics that are currently not the top priority in inappropriate situations. If, however, he becomes too absorbed in a topic and loses the connection with reality and the case at hand it also happens that his interlocutors simply leave. For him it is just hard to see how these social conditions work and he does not understand why the things floating around in his head are not the most important in the moment. Writer Sharon Lee Watson once confirmed the conjecture by writing "I think he has Asperger's. But that just makes him more loveable"[19]. Which suggests that the writers have only given Doctor Spencer Reid this psychological disorder, so his character looks clumsy and thus closer to the viewer as a completely perfect genius.

4. Comparison
4.1 Similarities between Spencer Reid and a typical genius
4.1.1 Considering the general definition

To begin with the first definition of genius Lewis Madison Terman would define Doctor Spencer Reid as a genius as one could expect his above-average properties like his "IQ of 187, [his] eidetic memory and [his ability to] read 20.000 words per minute"[20] to demonstrate his great intelligence with the help of a standardized intelligence test. Spencer would stand out from the crowd because his vast knowledge is almost all-encompassing compared to the limited knowledge of the average population. However, as Sir Francis Galton has defined the term genius in a more common variant the aspect of creativity must be considered as demonstrated by achievement. At this point one could argue two things since the creative aspect can be seen as a parallel between the typical genius and Doctor Spencer Reid on the one hand, because he invented this special and individual way of investigation and thus proved his creative ability in the regard. On the other hand there are differences between Spencer Reid and a typical genius when the argument of creativity is conceived in a different way since Spencer Reid discovers or researches nothing new beyond the bounds of his profession. Nevertheless, one can also say that Spencer has the ability of thinking beyond the borders for example when he breaks out of his prefabricated investigation pattern since he has noticed that it is smarter to think "outside

---

[19] Watson, Sharon Lee, "Criminal Minds Live Chat Transcript",
http://cmsetreport.tumblr.com/post/34127594413/full-transcript-live-chat-with-writer-sharon released on 18.10.2012, accessed on 27.10.2018
[20] Criminal Minds, Season 1, Episode 1, 11:00

the box"[21]. Another overlap of Spencer Reid and the typical genius is that a genius is not afraid of accepting the fact he does not know everything. And this is the way one can see Spencer Reid, because he told Special Agent Derek Morgan that he does not "know everything. I mean, despite the fact that you think that I do"[22]. This suggests that he knows society thinks he is omniscient, but he realizes that he does not know everything and has no fears to admit that. Moreover, he knows he has the opportunity to expand and to acquire further knowledge at any time by the fact that he only has to read information once to be able to access it in his memory at any time.

4.1.2 Considering the historical meaning
To refer Doctor Spencer Reid to the genius model of Johann Caspar Lavater it is also important to mention that this invisible creature of a higher kind dictating a genius how to behave, is also available in Criminal Minds. It is never obvious, but when Spencer Reid talks to a criminal who hears a voice which is telling him to kill people, Spencer admits that he "know[s] what the voices are like"[23]. In addition, Spencer knows that "they won't stop. They've been talking to you since you were a child"[24] which suggests that he is still hearing these voices. And just like Johann Caspar Lavater's descriptions, this voice has a positive impact on Spencer because "it's where you get your ideas from"[25] and

> "while the other kids were outside in the playground, you were inside reading, studying, learning. The voices wouldn't stop. They helped you understand things that other people could never realise and then as you grow older, it became almost a responsibility. A responsibility to use that ability. To use your knowledge"[26].

With this statement he affirms that his ideas and thought process was influenced by these voices and when they helped him understand things better than other people could he knew he had to use that gift and acted the way the voices influenced him. That is the point when Johann Caspar Lavater would define Spencer Reid as a genius, because he acts as if he was a being of a higher kind. Through these voices he has access to another level of knowledge and is therefore at the illustration of the schema on a higher level than the normal population with its limited

---

[21] Criminal Minds, Season 1, Episode 2, 25:55
[22] Criminal Minds, Season 1, Episode 5, 12:40
[23] Criminal Minds, Season 1, Episode 9, 36:52
[24] Criminal Minds, Season 1, Episode 9, 37:00
[25] Criminal Minds, Season 1, Episode 9, 37:25
[26] Criminal Minds, Season 1, Episode 9, 37:30

knowledge. According to Johann Caspar Lavater Doctor Spencer Reid is on the level where he is equated with God and thus has unlimited knowledge. Furthermore, the intellectual habitudes like intelligence, speech faculty and judgement that define a genius are qualities Spencer Reid has.

4.1.3 Considering the current significance

Andreas Sentker's model claims that a genius is born with basic abilities such as intelligence or temperament which is also the case with Spencer Reid because he has unlearned abilities such as the eidetic memory he brought with him when he was born. However, the essential "ingredients" that make a human being a genius are education, creativity, inspiration, intuition, independence, persistence and luck. Spencer Reid must have a completed and comprehensive school education as he already holds 3 doctorates so the logical conclusion is that he is educated and thereby fulfils the first "ingredient". The next factors such as creativity, inspiration and intuition are again related to his profession, but these are missing in private life. Independence and persistence are characteristics that Spencer Reid has because he acts individually and mostly without the thinking of others. Reid is also ambitious when he wants to solve a case for example he only stops dealing with the evidence when he has a reasonable suspicion.

4.2 Differences between Spencer Reid and the typical genius

4.2.1 Considering the general definition

As already indicated according to the definition of Sir Francis Galton Spencer Reid would rather not be a genius since he lacks the creative part in connection with the achievement of new advances. A genius has the ability to think beyond what exists and to discover, invent or explore new things. However, one cannot attribute this skill to Spencer Reid since he either does not own it or does not need it within his profession. During the investigations he thinks beyond borders, but never to the extent that one could speak of undiscovered areas or of things that no one ever has thought of before. Within his profession he never comes in contact with the transcendent or undiscovered but has to deal exclusively with the already existing. Without this basic attitude of creative creation Spencer Reid will not make any innovative and new discoveries.

4.2.2 Considering the historical meaning

Lavater's definition includes an enumeration of properties that define a genius. The perception, the sensation, the thinking, the speaking, the acting, the education, the poetry, the singing, the comparing, the special, the unification, the reasoning, the punishing and the giving and taking are different areas in which a person must be like a being of a higher kind to be considered as genius. The emotional traits such as sensation are not strong in Spencer Reid as he finds it difficult to show empathy and described himself as "insensitive"[27]. Moreover, he also struggles with ordering his feelings for example after he shot a criminal he mentions that he "know[s] [he] should feel bad about what happened. [He] killed a man. [He] should feel something. But [he does not]"[28]. Creative and artist qualities such as poetry, singing and creating are also not given since these are not necessary in his profession and are not mentioned in his private life. The social characteristics such as giving and taking could be given if Spencer Reid did not have Social Awkwardness which makes communication and interaction difficult for him. Arguing in this way leads to the solution that Spencer Reid has only intellectual competences and is therefore not considered a genius in the other areas. In addition, Lavater states that a genius does not feel or think as society has taught him. However, it is noticeable that Spencer Reid adapts everything he gets taught or shown by the other Agents and especially everything Special Agent Jason Gideon does into his behaviour. He probably does this to improve himself and possibly also to think more normally, but with it a part of his individuality gets lost.

4.2.3 Considering the current significance

According to Andreas Sentker, Spencer Reid would not be a combination of the seven "ingredients" that it takes to be called a genius. Because the creativity and inspiration are essential characteristics that Spencer Reid never showed within the series and therefore does not possess in the eyes of the audience. Besides, he was once told that "hanging out with [him] could be really depressing"[29] which shows he does not inspire the people around him. Moreover, it is impossible to attribute to Spencer Reid that he would always be lucky because he has good and bad days like any normal person and not a lifelong run of luck. However, it must be noted that these "ingredients" are for people who are preparing to change the world. Referring to this aspect to Spencer Reid, it turns out that he is trying to improve the world through his work by fighting evil, but not trying to change the world on a large scale.

---

[27] Criminal Minds, Season 1, Episode 18, 17:23
[28] Criminal Minds, Season 1, Episode 6, 38:55
[29] Criminal Minds, Season 1, Episode 18, 24:30

4.3 Final word

Weighing the arguments for and against the description of Doctor Spencer Reid as a typical genius, it is difficult to find one clear result. When considering the different models of the genius one comes across different solutions and thus cannot give a concrete definition of Doctor Spencer Reid as a typical genius. It all depends on the argumentation and definition of the different influences because the typical genius despite extensive research is still a vague and fictional term. It would be unbelievably unlikely if a human being had this exact combination of traits that are described in the typical genius. So, one can say that probably no person will ever be a typical genius and that does not have to be something bad, because it shows that humanity has such a broad variability that probably no human being will ever be of this type. But even if one cannot say that he is a typical genius, it does not mean he cannot generally be a genius. To refer the term "typical" to a human being can only end this way, because no human being completely corresponds to a typical cliché. If the writer of Criminal Minds had made Doctor Spencer Reid an unattainable and perfect genius, without his natural and human mistakes, his character could hardly be so sympathetic. Every person is different and individual and for the audience it is certainly nice to see that such an intelligent person also has his quirks and it would not fit his character traits if he suddenly created creative, artistic or inspiring works. Doctor Spencer Reid lives for his profession and gives everything to catch criminals and help victims. His goal is to use his mind and ingenious skills to make the world a better place and to fight for justice. In my opinion that may not make him a typical genius, but for sure an extraordinary hero.

5. References

Book sources:

Deutschbuch 10. Klasse Gymnasium Bayern

9. Sturm und Drang – Junge Stimmen gegen Autoritäten

9.1 Wie man sich selbst inszenieren kann – Der Geniekult des Sturm und Drang

Johann Caspar Lavater: Physiognomische Fragmente

Publishing Company: © 2008 Cornelsen Verlag, Berlin

Publisher: Wilhelm Matthiessen, Bernd Schurf und Wieland Zirbs

Authors: Gertraud Fuchsberger-Zirbs, Martin Hahn, Winfried Kober et al.

Internet sources:

Website author: BrainyMedia Inc, 2018

"Bernard Williams Quotes"

Date of access: 28.10.2018

https://www.brainyquote.com/quotes/bernard_williams_379649

Author: Kerr, Barbara

"Genius"

Date of release: 20.07.1998

Date of access: 11.10.2018

https://www.britannica.com/science/genius-psychology

Author: Sentker, Andreas

"Genial!" - Große Geister fallen nicht vom Himmel. Sieben Zutaten sind nötig, um Weltveränderer zu werden.

From the "Zeit" number 42/2011

Date of release: 13.10.2011

Date of access: 24.09.2018

https://www.zeit.de/2011/42/Genie-Kult/komplettansicht

Website author: 2018 Autism Speaks Inc.

"What is Autism?" - There is no one type of autism, but many.

Date of access: 27.10.2018

https://www.autismspeaks.org/what-autism

Website author: ©1996-2018 MedicineNet, Inc.

"Medical Definition of Asperger syndrome"

Date of review: 25.01.2017

Date of access: 27.10.2018

https://www.medicinenet.com/script/main/art.asp?articlekey=9675#aspergers_syndrome_fact s

Author: Watson, Sharon Lee

"Criminal Minds Live Chat Transcript"

Date of release: 18.10.2012

Date of access: 27.10.2018

http://cmsetreport.tumblr.com/post/34127594413/full-transcript-live-chat-with-writer-sharon

Series sources:

Criminal Minds

Season 1

Director: Charles Haid

Main actors: Mandy Patinkin, Thomas Gibson and Lola Glaudini

Supporting actors: Shemar Moore, Matthew Gray Gubler, Kirsten Vangness and A. J. Cook

Date of release: 01.01.2005

Film studio: ABC Studios

YOUR KNOWLEDGE HAS VALUE

- We will publish your bachelor's and master's thesis, essays and papers

- Your own eBook and book - sold worldwide in all relevant shops

- Earn money with each sale

Upload your text at www.GRIN.com
and publish for free